I0814878

Idaho

BY IB LARSEN

An Imprint of Abdo Publishing
abdobooks.com

abdobooks.com

Published by Abdo Publishing, a division of ABDO, PO Box 398166, Minneapolis, Minnesota 55439. Copyright © 2025 by Abdo Consulting Group, Inc. International copyrights reserved in all countries. No part of this book may be reproduced in any form without written permission from the publisher. Kids Core™ is a trademark and logo of Abdo Publishing.

Printed in China.
052024
092024

Cover Photo: Charles Knowles/Shutterstock Images
Interior Photo: Keystone-France/Gamma-Keystone/Getty Images, 4–5; Double Brow Imagery/Shutterstock Images, 7 (top left); Bob Gibbons/Alamy, 7 (top right); Shutterstock Images, 7 (bottom left), 8, 10, 18, 22, 24; Dmitriy Gutkovskiy/Shutterstock Images, 7 (bottom right); August Frank/Lewiston Tribune/AP Images, 12–13; IanDagnall Computing/Alamy, 14; Gerald Corsi/iStockphoto, 17; Charles Knowles/Shutterstock Images, 20–21; JMY Photography/Shutterstock Images, 23; Jef Wodniack/Shutterstock Images, 26; Loren Orr/NASCAR/Getty Images, 28 (Meridian); Jerome A. Pollos/Coeur d'Alene Press/AP Images, 28 (Silverwood); CS Nafzger/Shutterstock Images, 28 (Sun Valley); Red Line Editorial, 28 (map), 29

Editor: Christa Kelly
Series Designer: Katharine Hale

Library of Congress Control Number: 2023949406

Publisher's Cataloging-in-Publication Data

Names: Larsen, Ib, author.
Title: Idaho / by Ib Larsen
Description: Minneapolis, Minnesota: Abdo Publishing, 2025 | Series: Discovering the United States | Includes online resources and index.
Identifiers: ISBN 9781098293826 (lib. bdg.) | ISBN 9798384913092 (ebook)
Subjects: LCSH: U.S. states--Juvenile literature. | Idaho--History--Juvenile literature. | Western States (U.S.)--Juvenile literature. | Physical geography--United States--Juvenile literature.
Classification: DDC 973--dc23

All population data taken from:
"Estimates of Population by Sex, Race, and Hispanic Origin: April 1, 2020 to July 1, 2022." *US Census Bureau, Population Division,* June 2023, census.gov.

CONTENTS

Sun Valley Resort was created by the Union Pacific Railroad to encourage people to take trains.

CHAPTER 1

The World's First Ski Chairlift

It was December 1936. Skiers stood at the base of Proctor Mountain in Idaho. The Sun Valley Resort was about to open the world's first ski chairlift. Skiers had always had to climb the mountain themselves. The chairlift changed this.

Now, skiers could relax as a chair hanging from a cable carried them up the slopes.

The first skiers got on the lift. They sat 20 feet (6 m) above the ground. Passengers were given blankets to keep them warm during the slow ride. The chairlift carried the skiers 1,150 feet (351 m) to the top of the mountain. The invention was a success!

The Sun Valley Resort is still open today. People can visit Proctor Mountain to see where the first chairlift used to be. It is one of the many fun places to visit in Idaho.

Idaho's Land

Idaho is in the United States region called the West. To Idaho's north is Canada. Nevada and

Idaho Facts

DATE OF STATEHOOD
July 3, 1890

CAPITAL
Boise

POPULATION
1,939,033

AREA
83,569 square miles (216,443 sq km)

STATE BIRD

Mountain bluebird

STATE TREE

Western white pine

STATE FLOWER

Syringa

STATE VEGETABLE

Potato

Each US state has a different population, size, and capital city. States also have state symbols.

Utah are to its south. Idaho shares its western border with Oregon and Washington. Montana and Wyoming are to the east.

Idaho has black bears, *pictured*, and grizzly bears.

Idaho has many **biomes**. The state is covered in forests, grasslands, deserts, and mountains. Bighorn sheep and cougars live in the mountains. One of Idaho's most famous mountain ranges is the Lost River Range.

Borah Peak is part of this range. The peak is the highest point in Idaho.

Almost two-fifths of the state is covered in forests. The forests are made up of pine, fir, and maple trees. These forests provide homes for Idaho's wildlife. This includes bears, gray wolves, and caribou.

Earthquake

In 1983, an earthquake struck central Idaho. It was the largest earthquake recorded in Idaho's history. It was so powerful that it raised the height of Borah Peak by about 1 foot (0.3 m). **Aftershocks** occurred for several months.

Idaho has more than 100 mountain ranges.

Idaho's Climate

Idaho has four seasons. Temperatures throughout the year depend on **elevation**. Idaho's mountains have cooler temperatures than the rest of the state. They often get rain and snow. The parts of the state at lower elevations get very little rain and snow. This is because the mountains lining the eastern part of the state block most of the clouds.

Further Evidence

Look at the website below. Does it give any new evidence to support Chapter One?

Idaho

abdocorelibrary.com/discovering-idaho

There are more than 3,500 registered members of the Nez Perce nation.

CHAPTER 2

The People of Idaho

The first people arrived in Idaho about 10,000 years ago. They were American Indians. Over time, nations developed. These nations include the Shoshone and the Nez Perce. The Shoshone people are native to southern Idaho. They used to hunt bison.

It took more than a year for Meriwether Lewis, *left*, and William Clark, *right*, to travel from Missouri to Oregon.

The Nez Perce are native to northern Idaho. Some weave bags out of corn husks.

In 1805, Meriwether Lewis and William Clark became the first white explorers in Idaho.

President Thomas Jefferson sent them to explore the territory. They crossed the continent from Missouri to Oregon, passing through Idaho on the way.

Many of Idaho's early white settlers were fur traders and **missionaries**. Gold was discovered in northern Idaho in 1860. This brought many people from other states.

Sacagawea

Sacagawea was a Shoshone woman from what is now Idaho. Lewis and Clark hired her white Canadian husband as a guide. She came with him. Her knowledge of the land and the local Shoshone and Hidatsa languages helped Lewis and Clark explore Idaho.

Today, about 80 percent of Idaho's population is white. About 13.5 percent is Hispanic or Latino. Almost 2 percent is American Indian. Another 2 percent is Asian. About 1 percent is Black.

Culture

Food is an important part of Idaho's culture. Many Idaho dishes contain potatoes. Potato pancakes are made by flattening and then frying potatoes.

Finger steaks are another popular Idaho dish. They are made by deep frying seasoned strips of beef steak. Huckleberries are another classic food from Idaho. People use the berries to make jam and ice cream.

Huckleberries grow at mid to high elevations.

Farmers in Idaho harvest 13 billion pounds (6 trillion kg) of potatoes every year.

Outdoor activities are also important parts of Idaho's culture. Many people enjoy camping and hiking in the state's forests. Others visit Idaho's rivers to fish and raft. During the winter, they ski and snowshoe.

Industries

Many people in Idaho are farmers. They grow crops and raise animals such as cattle and sheep. Potatoes are among the state's most popular crops. Idaho produces one-third of the potatoes grown in the United States.

Some people in Idaho have jobs cutting down trees for wood. Others turn this wood into furniture and other products.

Explore Online

Visit the website below. Does it give any new information about Idaho that wasn't in Chapter Two?

Hello from Idaho!

abdocorelibrary.com/discovering-idaho

Boise, Idaho, has a population of more than 200,000.

Places in Idaho

Boise is the capital of Idaho. It is also the state's most **populated** city. In 2022, Boise was one of the fastest-growing cities in the United States. The city has a popular zoo called Zoo Boise. It is home to lions, giraffes, and monkeys.

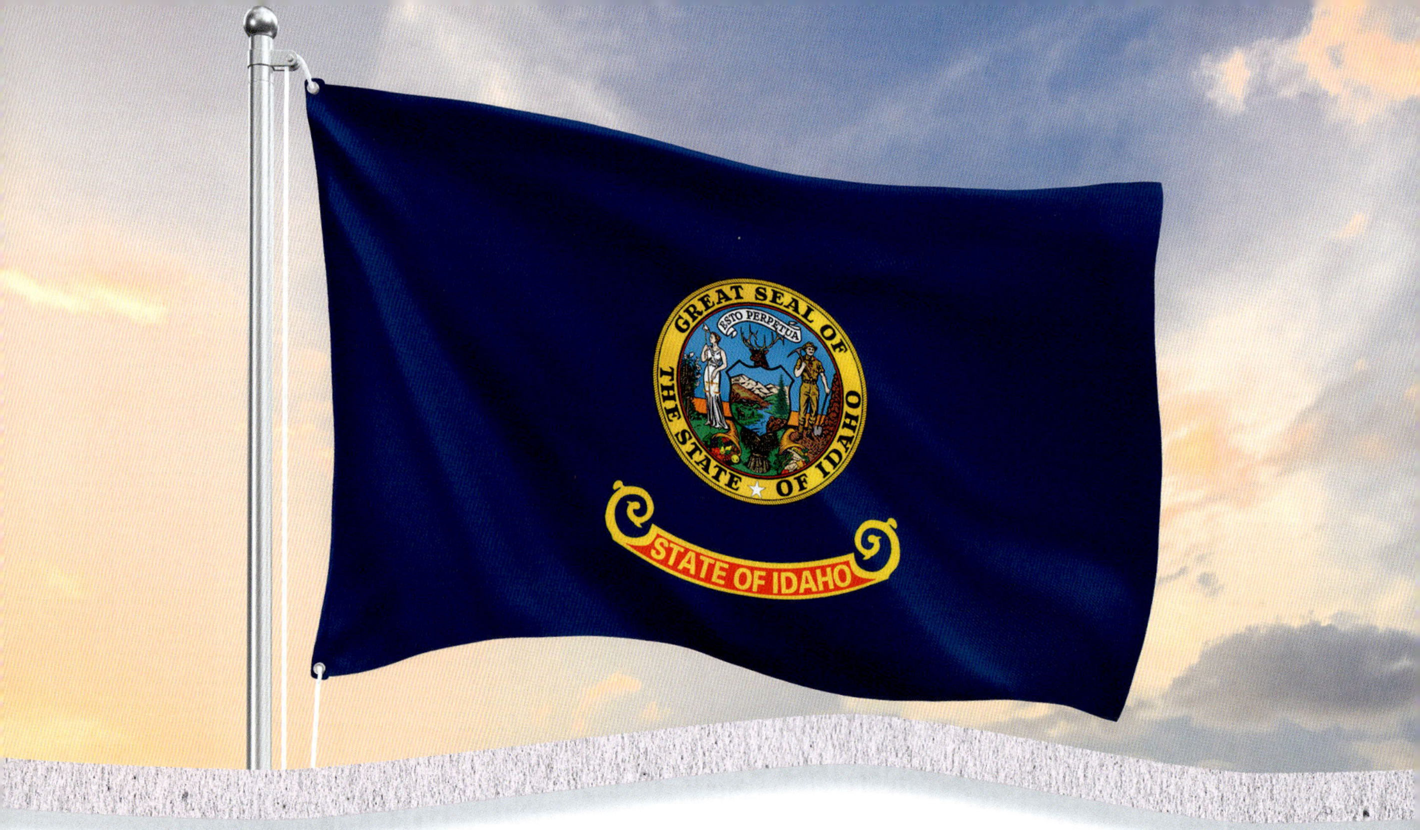

The current Idaho flag was created in 1957.

Meridian is Idaho's second most populated city. The city has 24 parks. It's also home to the Meridian Speedway. The speedway is a famous car racing track.

Parks and Nature

Idaho has several nationally protected sites. Craters of the Moon National Monument

Craters of the Moon formed during volcanic activity between 2,000 and 15,000 years ago.

and Preserve is named for its otherworldly landscape. Fields of black rocks left by cooling lava cover the land. Visitors can hike the park's trails and learn about the land's volcanic history.

Nez Perce National Historical Park is made up of several Nez Perce sites across Idaho and other states. These sites include battlefields, prairies, and ancient villages. Visitors can learn about the history of the Nez Perce people.

The water that flows down the cliffs at Thousand Springs State Park comes from underground.

Idaho also has many state parks. At Thousand Springs State Park, visitors can watch springs flow out of the sides of cliffs. Farragut State Park is on the southern part of Lake Pend Oreille. Hiking, biking, and boating are popular activities for park visitors.

Landmarks

Many people visit Idaho to see its landmarks. One such landmark is the Perrine Bridge. The bridge is located in southern Idaho. It crosses Snake River **Canyon**.

The Warhawk Air Museum is in western Idaho. Visitors can tour the massive museum.

Snake River Canyon

Snake River Canyon is about 1,320 feet (400 m) wide. In 1974, stunt performer Evel Knievel tried to cross the canyon in a small rocket. He shot 1,000 feet (300 m) into the air, but his parachute went off early. He landed uninjured in the canyon. In 2016, another stunt performer, Eddie Braun, completed the jump.

Some people jump off Perrine Bridge with parachutes as part of a sport called BASE jumping.

They can see planes used in World War I (1914–1918) and World War II (1939–1945).

Silverwood Theme Park is located in Athol in northern Idaho. It has more than 70 rides and attractions for all ages of visitors. Visitors can ride on a steam engine train and a Ferris wheel. They can also drive **antique** cars!

Idaho has beautiful parks and landmarks. It also has a fascinating history. Everyone can find something to love about Idaho.

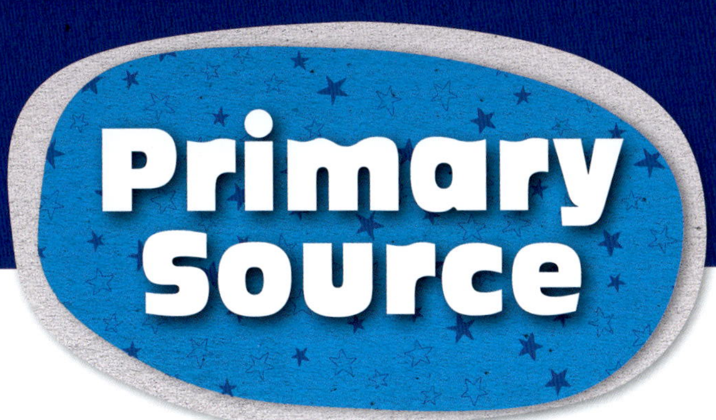

Kurt Ikeda was a park ranger at Craters of the Moon. He talked about the park's history:

> Many people have come to this wonderland of lava. . . . The **ancestors** of the Shoshone and Bannock tribes traveled through here thousands of years ago. Folks on the Oregon Trail came by in the mid 1800s. And in 1969, astronauts from Apollo 14 were also here.

Source: "Become a Virtual Junior Ranger." *National Park Service*, n.d., nps.gov. Accessed 17 Oct. 2023.

What's the Big Idea?

Read this quote. What is its main idea? Explain how the main idea is supported by details.

State Map

KEY

Capital
Park
City or town
Point of interest

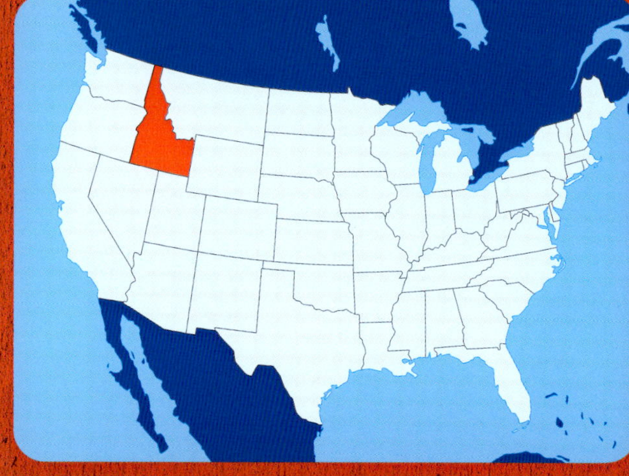

Meridian Speedway

Silverwood Theme Park

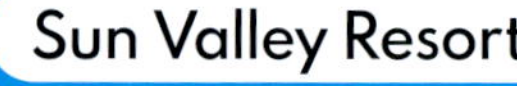

Sun Valley Resort

Idaho: The Gem State

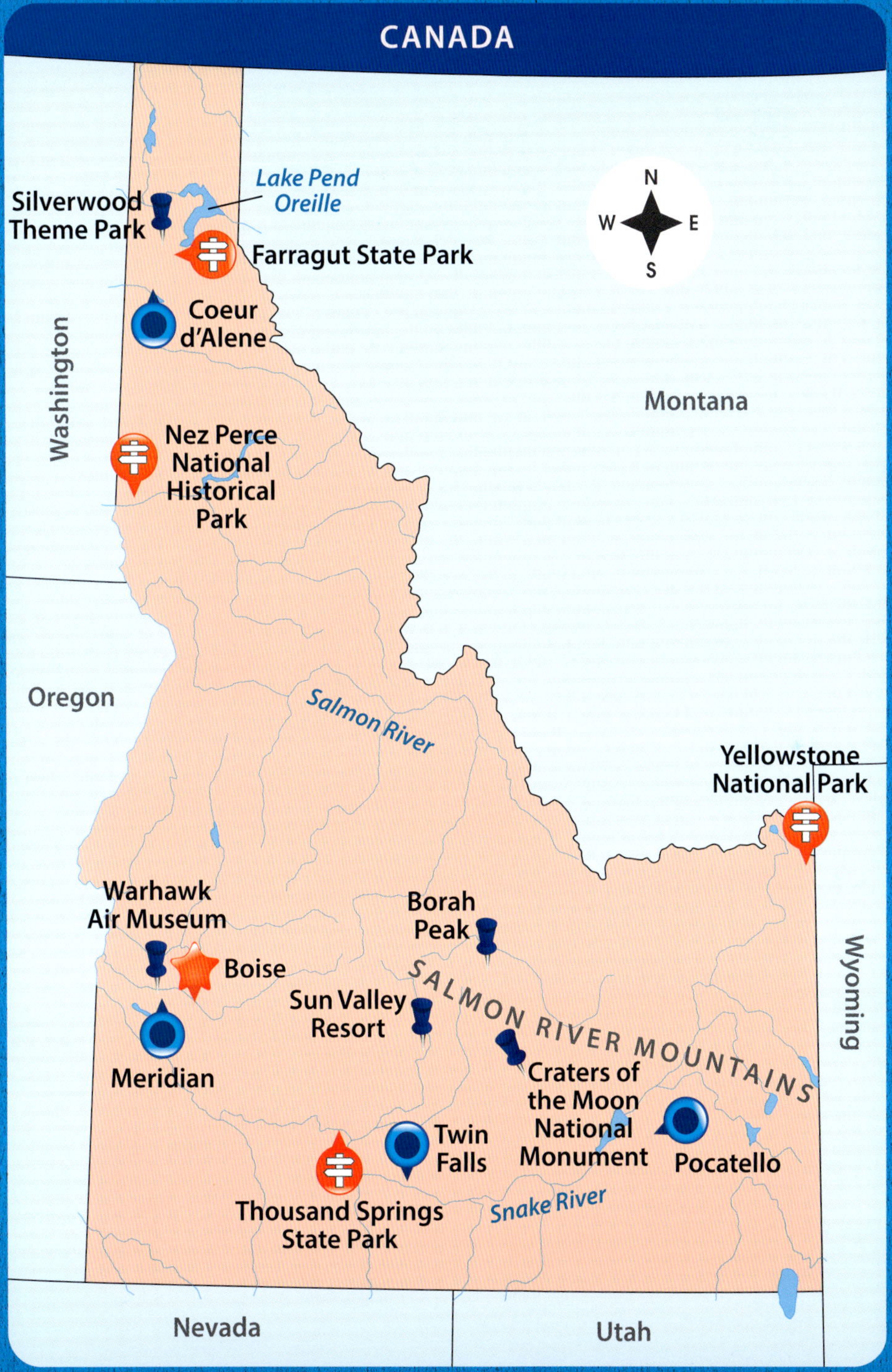

Glossary

aftershocks
smaller earthquakes that occur after a larger one

ancestors
the people from whom a person is descended and who lived many generations ago

antique
very old and human-made

biomes
land areas with their own climates, plants, and animals

canyon
a deep, narrow valley cut by a river through rock

elevation
the height above sea level

missionaries
people who travel to other lands to spread their religion

populated
settled or lived in

Online Resources

To learn more about Idaho, visit our free resource websites below.

Visit **abdocorelibrary.com** or scan this QR code for free Common Core resources for teachers and students, including vetted activities, multimedia, and booklinks, for deeper subject comprehension.

Visit **abdobooklinks.com** or scan this QR code for free additional online weblinks for further learning. These links are routinely monitored and updated to provide the most current information available.

Learn More

Bird, F. A. *Nez Perce*. Abdo, 2022.

Platt, Christine. *Sacagawea*. Magic Wagon, 2020.

Tieck, Sarah. *Idaho*. Abdo, 2020.

Index

About the Author

Ib Larsen is a writer and editorial assistant living in Saint Paul, Minnesota.